The Basic Essentials of
Backpacking

by Harry Roberts

Globe Pequot Press
Old Saybrook, Connecticut

THE BASIC ESSENTIALS OF BACKPACKING

Dedication

To Cliff Jacobson, who pestered me from 1979 to 1987 to edit *Canoeing Magazine*, and who pestered me since 1987 to write another book. He made it happen, folks. Blame me if there's blame. Thank him if there's praise.

Library of Congress Cataloging-in-Publication Data

Roberts, Harry.
    Backpacking--the basic essentials.

    (The Basic essentials series)
    Includes index.
    1. Backpacking.   2. Backpacking--Equipment and supplies.   I. Title.
GV199.6.R6   1989   796.5'1'028   88-34802
ISBN 0-934802-44-0

TABLE OF CONTENTS

1. PRELIMINARY CHIRK

It's always struck me as strange to start a book on any activity, be it gourmet cooking or model railroading, with a long, passionate bleat about how much FUN it is. It'd seem only reasonable to assume that you, the reader, bought the book in the first place to read about something that you already figured would be fun in the first place. I mean, when was the last time you bought a book about hitting your thumb with a clawhammer?

Agreed, then ... backpacking, and its less strenuous cousin, walking in the woods, is fun. My job here is not to tell you that it's fun. It's to show you how to do some things when you're out there that'll *keep* it fun for you, your family and your friends.

Let's run through that last sentence again. My job is to show you how to do some things. My job is not to tell you to buy some things. You'll need some gear, no doubt. And you may need some words of commonsense advice about choosing gear. But I've always felt that if you understand the demands placed on equipment, and how to use that equipment, you can make informed decisions for yourself. The most expensive gear in the outdoor sports shop is most frequently the best gear available; this is still an honest game, in which you get what you pay for. But you'll still sleep cold in your top-of-the-line down bag if you don't know how to sleep in a sleeping bag. And I don't care how light each one of those wonderful little gadgets is that you're carrying around to make your life comfortable out there. They still have to be carried around on your back, and your back can't tell the difference between thirty extra pounds of the best superlight toys and thirty pounds of lutefisk.

Don't get me wrong. I like toys; I like neat things that work. But all the neat toys in the store won't keep you as warm, dry and generally comfortable as will a few ounces of knowledge.

That's my sermon for today. Let's take a walk in the woods!

GETTING STARTED

If you think of it as *"backpacking,"* you'll get your head screwed on wrong from the start, because backpacking has had a wealth of connotations grow up about it that have no place in the real world out there.

When you take a walk in the woods for a day, you take some of your closet and some of the kitchen with you. When you take a walk in the woods for more than a day, you have to take the bedroom with you, and a little more of the kitchen. That's all. All backpacking is in terms of gear is dayhiking with a bedroom. This both cuts away a lot of precious nonsense and also leaves you receptive to some ideas about straightforward, functional gear selection and use.

You start in backpacking by taking a walk in the woods. After a lot of walks in the woods, you start to get very comfortable out there, and you almost resent walking back out to your car. You'd like to stay the night, so you could see more and be out there longer. Then — and only then — is when you consider backpacking.

Until that time, you're just taking walks in the woods. You can glorify those walks by telling your friends that you're going hiking — but there are few uglier words than *"hiking"* in the language. *"Hiking"* is what you do with a field pack and an assault rifle in a swamp in South Carolina. *"Hiking"* is what you did as a

12-year old when you refused to believe that you could survive a night in the woods without a portable radio, five changes of clothing, four pounds of Oreos, a 12-inch cast iron frypan, an 11-pound sleeping bag, and three 40-ounce bottles of RC Cola. *"Hiking"* is what you do when the manager comes to the mound and asks for the ball because you've just given up six straight extra-base hits. *"Take a hike, son."* Sure.

You can take a hike if you wish. I'll take a walk in the woods.

And any woods will do.

In fact, you don't even need woods. Open country's just fine. It doesn't have to be in the Smokies or the Ozarks or the Sierras or the Adirondacks or the Whites. It doesn't have to be famous or glamorous or written about in ecosport magazines. It simply has to be there, be close by, and be public. This may seem to be terribly obvious when it's put down here in plain old black-and-white, but it isn't obvious to a whole lot of people, who stay at home and dream about distant vistas when they could be out and about at home.

Don't get trapped by the exotic. Don't dream so much about the Wonderland Trail that circumnavigates Mount Rainier that you forget the wonderland next door.

How To Walk. Huh? *"But I know how to walk!,"* you say. I can't argue with that. But most people, who otherwise walk reasonably well, take some notion of how they should walk with a pack to heart, and wind up expending vast amounts of energy with little return for it.

To begin with, the woods walker, with or without a pack, is more often than not on irregular terrain, where balance is a bit more of a problem. Add to that the fact of a pack, and you find that you're simply not quite as catty in the outback as you are on a gym floor. Rule One? Shorten your stride. Keep your feet under you.

Rule Two? Walk erect. I know; this isn't always easy on a trail. But the more erect you are, the easier it is to carry a load, the more comfortable the pack will be, and the happier your back will be. If you find yourself slumping, carry a staff or a long walking stick. And try this gimmick when you have to go up a sharp little hill — or one of those interminable, not-steep-enough-to-rest-on-but-too-steep-for-comfort grinds that take you up 1000 feet per mile. Straighten up, shorten your stride, pause for a split second before you push yourself uphill with each stride, and *walk with your hands on your hips.* I've never taken the time to investigate just why this works, but it does. Try it.

And that's it. Go walk somewhere with your house on your back!

ATTITUDES

There's nothing you need to learn about functioning easily and happily in the outback that can't be learned with very little difficulty. Being comfortable in good weather and making do in bad is, after all, a game that rewards attention to detail rather than an intelligence rating that qualifies for you Mensa. In short, it's a game that most people can learn.

What is somewhat less predictable is the set of attitudes you bring to the game. It's those attitudes that ultimately determine whether or not you'll enjoy it out there — and, more to the point, whether anybody travelling with you will enjoy it.

Start with this. Tattoo it on the back of your right hand if your memory is poor. Just don't forget it.

I AM NOT HERE TO CONQUER ANYTHING

If you still have room on your hand, put this on it now.

THE SLOWEST PERSON IN THIS PARTY IS WORKING AS HARD AS I AM

Now put this on the back of your left hand.

A TRAIL IS NOT A COMBAT ZONE

Okay. You can go out there now.

2. FIRST STEPS

There aren't many places in North America that don't have some sort of public parkland nearby. It may be a county park, a state park, a provincial park in Canada, a state forest, a Nature Conservancy area or even a National Park or National Forest. Whatever it's called, it's a place to take a walk in the woods.

How do you find places like this?

The easiest way is to pick up the telephone book, turn to the Yellow Pages, and look under Camping Equipment, Sporting Goods, or Mountain Climbing Equipment and make a few telephone calls. Discard any shops that answer with something like *"Uh, well, hey, nobody walks any more. Wanna buy a four-wheeler cheap?,"* and in time, you'll find a shop that sells hiking and backpacking gear. That's where the information is. Go to this store and ask the friendly folks who work there about local public lands. They'll know. They'll also know how to work you quickly through the switchboard of the state agency that deals with outdoor recreation, which may have a misleading name like Department of Game and Fish or Department of Environmental Conservation, but which will have, somewhere in its innards, a group that oversees walking, canoeing and ski touring trails. It'll probably be called Forest Recreation. It will have some publications and maps available, and it will be understaffed, so don't expect them to fit boots for you or find the perfect backcountry hidey-hole for you.

Your favorite local outdoor outfitter will have detailed maps of popular trails in your area. If you're going to consider walking a trail in another state or county; check with a local outdoor store for maps and advice. You might find that what looked good on the map sent from the State Park doesn't discuss the all-terrain-vehicle trail that runs along side the "27 mile nature trail." There's nothing worse than traveling 250 miles with the intention of walking into solitude and finding your "nature trail" is a-buzz with Honda RM 250's tearing through the State Forest.

This atrocity can be avoided by a call to a local outfitting store. If a store is not in the area, consult the town's Bureau of Tourism. A well made map can help, however, even the finest maps will not warn you about a problem like a noisy motorcycle trail.

Here are a few addresses for some top quality topographic maps. The National Cartographic Information Center (N.C.I.C.) will help you find special purpose maps of all kinds. It sorts and collects cartographic information from Federal, State and local government agencies. Write the N.C.I.C. office nearest you for a listing of city, county and wilderness area (U.S. national parks and forest) maps and aerial photos, and more. N.C.I.C. will answer all your map questions ... and sell you what you need. They have a ton of free pamphlets.

N.C.I.C. Headquarters
National Cartographic Information Center
U.S. Geological Survey
507 National Center
Reston, VA 22092

Western Mapping Center, N.C.I.C.
U.S. Geological Survey
345 Middlefield Rd.
Menlo Park, CA 94025

Rocky Mountain Mapping Center, N.C.I.C.
U.S. Geological Survey, Box 25046
Denver, Federal Center, Mail Stop 504
Denver, CO 80225

Midcontinent Mapping Center, N.C.I.C.
U.S. Geological Survey
1400 Independence Rd.
Rolla, MO 65401

Order Canadian topographic maps, Land Use Information Series maps and aerial photos from:

Canada Map Office
Dept. of Energy, Mines and Resources
615 Booth St.
Ottawa, Ontario KIA OE9

For Canadian charts and tide tables:

Hydrographic Chart Distribution Office
Dept. of Fisheries and Oceans
1675 Russel Rd., P.O. Box 8080
Ottawa, Ontario K1G 3H6

Now you're armed with a lot of information about where to go. Some of it looks absolutely compelling. Some of it looks pretty esoteric. Some of it deals with unappetizing places like swamps. In time, you'll turn a back somersault and shout *"Hallelujah"* when you find a new swamp. Right off the bat, you'll probably shudder and pass on the wetlands. That's all right. You'll learn.

Now, let's go back to those pleasant people who work at the shop that sells backpacking gear, and make a few small purchases. If you'll be walking in the woods by yourself, go alone. If you're walking with your family, take your family. I say this as a grizzled veteran Spouse, Dad and Grandfather. Take the family!

BUT WHERE TO WALK?
BASIC TRIP PLANNING.

It should be obvious that we're not going to plan your first trip right here. But we're going to talk over a few notions that should make your first trip — and all other trips — easier and more pleasurable for you. Because the *"planning"* we're talking about here is planning for terrain.

The last time you were at your friendly local outfitter's, you heard some veteran backpackers talking about what they called a neat, easy weekend trip. Hey! Just the thing for you and your spouse and the 10-year old! So ... you pick up the trail map and the guidebook to the trail systems in the Pellagra State Wilderness, and charge on home with the good news.

"Yep! Here it is! You start out at the Blackfly Brook parking area, go eleven miles — really only ten-point-seven-three miles — across Toothache Ridge and Blister Butte to Dead Hiker Clearing. That's not bad at all. We walked about twelve miles last Saturday, and it was a piece of cake!"

Yep. It *was* a piece of cake. Flatland walking on old tote roads, carrying a seven-pound day pack. A *lovely* piece of cake, and well within your capacities. The walk to Dead Hiker Clearing might be shorter, but let's look at the guide book and the map some more.

Hmmm. It looks like seven of those miles are going either up or down at a rate close to 1000 feet per mile. The rest of it looks to be fairly easy, except the terrain between Toothache Ridge and Blister Butte is rocky, and it has been raining lately.

Hmmm. This isn't exactly a tote road in the jackpine flats of the Huron National Forest. Let's think about this one. In fact, let's start to divide the whole world of backpacking up into Easy, Moderate and Severe Terrain. That way, we can remove the discussion from what I think is easy or what you think is easy.

Easy Terrain. Easy terrain is flat, or nearly so, and the footing is secure. A bog is flat — but there's no way you can relax and let out your stride. Soft sand may be better — but not much. Forest roads, trails following streams that don't come downhill at a severe rate, rolling hills — these are generally easy walking, and you can

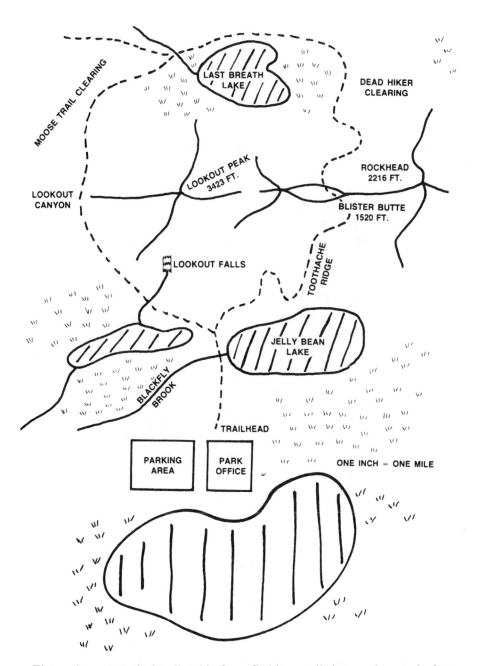

Figure 1   A typical trail guide for a fictitious trail that can be acquired at the trailhead office. Always consider terrain and elevation; it looks like a short 11 mile walk, but the terrain and elevation makes it more difficult.

plan for two miles an hour, including breaks. Sure, you could go faster, but why bother? If you want to race, take up race walking, where everybody is competing *and knows it.* Don't inflict a sneaky sort of competition on your companions when they know neither the game nor the rules.

Moderate Terrain. I have a tendency to call easy terrain *"moderate"* when I'm dealing with novices, unless they're gorillas, because if you haven't backpacked, no terrain is really easy. However, to quantify *"moderate,"* I'd call it a trail that's mostly solid underfoot, with either one pretty stiff hill in it somewhere, or a series of little hitchetybops, of the sort that are great when you're on a well-groomed track and your skis are running but which are less than a Sardukar's idea of Paradise on foot.

You can charge along and still make two miles an hour, but best figure 1.5 miles per hour. This lets you stop to smell the roses.

Which brings up another point. Even if you're tired, you're better off to walk steadily and fall into a mindless rhythm, stopping for long enough to refresh yourself, rather than drag along and never stop. Smell the roses, by all means. But take the time to smell them thoroughly, and then let yourself become absorbed in the simple and joyful act of walking.

Severe Terrain. Any terrain in which you ascend or descend over 500 feet in a mile of trail is severe. And don't let any Trail Animal convince you otherwise. When you know the game better, you'll question this statement, too. But don't question it now, don't question it ever in public, and don't question it ever when you talk to people backpacking as a family.

The fact is that most trails in mountainous country ascend and descend at about 1000 feet per mile, which is like climbing a long, gentle staircase, except it will vary from flat or nearly so to places where there may literally be ladders to scale. Western trails, which have frequently been designed to accommodate horses, are generally less steep, but take a lot longer to get to where they're going. Is ten miles of 500 feet per mile ascent worse than five miles of 1000 feet per mile ascent? I can't tell you. I know I'd rather descend the longer, gentler slope. Steep descents are as debilitating to your leg muscles as steep ascents, particularly when you're carrying your house on your back.

In severe terrain, plan on a mile an hour. You'll still have time to smell the roses — but you'll be huffin' and puffin' when you do.

With these measurements in mind, we see now that the jaunt back into Dead Hiker Clearing is no piece of cake. Seven miles of those are taken at one mph; three of them are taken at 1.5 mph; that's nine hours so far, and we still have that 0.73 miles to take care of. Okay, it's a piece of cake — but it's the last of the trail, and it takes an hour. That's ten hours of walking. That's too much right now. It may be too much anytime, unless it's a flatout emergency.

Were the folks back at your outfitter's pulling everybody's coat when they called it an easy jaunt? Maybe. There are some people — all of whom swear that they're not competitive — who'll brag on something like this. It's like the paddlers who call a solid Class IV drop a Class II, so when you eat it, they can posture and look like heroes. Sleaze is sleaze, friends. And no pastime, profession or social order is free of sleaze.

More than likely, though, you dropped in on the weekend warriors swapping stories with the shop people. These are hard people. They carry a minimum of very high quality, lightweight gear and they're in superb condition for backpacking. You'd find, if you asked them, that they're active all year round. They ski, they paddle, they ride bicycles. They're technicians in terms of learning proper techniques for biomechanical activities. They like to do things well. They probably blaze into Dead Hiker Clearing in five hours, smell all the roses on the way twice, stop for lunch and maybe even a few Z's, and get to the Clearing in time to scramble up the cirque wall on Blister Butte. They're for real.

And you know something? If you went backpacking with them, they'd travel at a pace comfortable for you. Remember that when you become a Certified Trail Animal. As the old-time horse players used to say, *"Class shows when there is no class."*

3. BASIC GEAR FOR WALKING IN THE WOODS

Check this chapter heading again, please. We're talking about walking in the woods. We're not talking about hero treks along the crest of the Continental Divide. When it's time to do that, you'll be writing your own book. But right now, we want to look over some gear that'll make your walk in the woods a pleasure — and that you won't *outgrow*.

Let's consider this a moment. When I talk about gear you won't outgrow, I'm not talking about size. I'm talking about quality. The old axiom that you buy cheap gear three or four times is never so true as it is with outdoor gear. Get a cheap pack if you wish; just be prepared for it to never work well, to never be comfortable, and to require replacement after only limited use. This isn't an argument for buying the top-of-the-line gear, with bells and whistles. The time may come when the bells and whistles are useful to you; for now, it's doubtful that you need a loop for your ice axe and straps for carrying crampons. What you're shopping for should fit well, look good (woodchucks to the contrary, pretty DOES count for something), and hold up in use.

What you're shopping for specifically are a few items that will make your life easier in the outback, and something in which to carry them. That *"something"* is commonly called a daybag, a day pack, or a small rucksack. And — surprise! — we're not going to talk about the pack first. Why? Because until you have a pretty good idea of what's going into the pack, the size and shape of the pack itself is absolutely meaningless.

You could probably make up a list of what you need for a day's walk in the woods in spring, summer or fall without my help if you thought about it for a minute, but I'll help you.

Water. This is the one indispensable item in any wilderness traveller's kit, for reasons that are both obvious and far too extensive to go into here. As you can't depend on finding drinkable water anywhere close to human habitation and only rarely out in the boondocks, you either go prepared to treat water to make it drinkable, or you carry water with you.

Figure 2   Wide-mouth backpacking water bottles are more suitable for backpacking than small-mouthed canteens.

For a short scoot in the woods, the simple approach is to carry water with you. So, you'll need something in which to carry it. Rummage through your outfitter's shelves until you find a wide-mouthed plastic bottle that will hold about a liter. I prefer water bottles made of Nalgene, because Nalgene doesn't pick up flavors as readily as some other plastics. Why a wide-mouth bottle rather than a narrow-mouthed canteen? Simple. It's easier to fill, and it's easier to mix stuff like lemonade in a wide-mouth bottle. Get one for every family member who's walking with you.

Food. If you aren't troubled with metabolic problems like diabetes or hypoglycemia, going a day without food will not hurt you a bit. However, this isn't the time to either go on a diet or start the practice of fasting.

It also isn't the time to go on a Sugar Junky binge, either. The mild exercise you get from walking will trigger a low-level release of stored glycogens from your liver after you've gone through the sugars in your bloodstream, so you don't need five pounds of chocolate bars.

Here's what I take. Cheese (usually a sharp cheddar), pepperoni or beef stick, a few Triscuits, a hard roll, and something sweet that won't melt. There IS chocolate that won't melt. It's called M & M's. Mix these gaudy little dudes with some dry roast peanuts in a ziploc bag, and you'll be good to go, as my old point guard was fond of saying.

Do yourself a favor. Buy a small plastic box that's sealable for the cheese and the pepperoni. You won't regret it — unless you really like your pack to smell of garlic.

Your favorite outdoor outfitter will have an assortment of freeze-dried and dehydrated food packets you might consider preparing. Sometimes the meals are extravagant but for the most part they are very easy to prepare. Again it is important to consult a helpful salesperson to get a little experienced advice.

The benefit in taking along freeze-dried and dehydrated fare is the weight difference of these products as opposed to that of groceries. With the water extracted from the food, weight load is reduced to more than fifty percent of the original weight. This is most important when cross country trekking, however, you might wish to make it easy on your back with the lightweight stuff.

Raingear. Chances are that it rains where you live. Chances are that it will rain on you sometime when you're moseying through the north forty. Most rational beings won't set out for a walk in the woods when the fall gales hit the upper Great Lakes, or the rains hit the Georgia coastal plains, but if you wait to walk for that perfect day when there is no threat of rain at all, you won't do much walking. You're not made of sugar; you won't melt.

But you'll think you're made of sugar if your raingear doesn't work well. Now, *"work well"* is one of those wonderful weasel phrases beloved of outdoor writers who either choose not to go into detail or don't spend enough time outside to know what's happening. Because — what works well today for me may not work well for you today, even if you're walking beside me.

Why? A lot of reasons. I may be expending a bit less energy, and perspiring less. I may be more comfortable on a hot, humid day, and because I'm fussing less, I'm less prone to being bothered by a little condensation. I may be walking with a thin polypropylene undershirt under my rain jacket, and you may have a heavy cotton/ poly blend t-shirt on, which traps moisture and makes you feel damp. I may have taken the time to ventilate trapped warm air from inside the jacket by loosening my collar, and I may have chosen to wear a hat rather than pull up the hood on my jacket, which effectively insulates the nape of my neck and my throat — two areas which are critical in heat regulation. In simpler terms, it's a combination of good raingear and good sense that keeps you comfortable. Good raingear alone makes the job easier, but it's no guarantee of comfort.

Raingear can be divided into two designs, the poncho and the commonly — used rain jacket/rain pants sets. The poncho is big, a pain the neck in a breeze, relatively easy to ventilate, and if you're looking for double-duty from your gear, downright hazardous in a canoe or on a bicycle. Rain jackets and rain pants are rather more versatile, require more care in use to maintain adequate ventilation, are more comfortable in a wind, and can, indeed, serve as wind garments. If I was limiting my outings to generally warm weather, and didn't want to spend a lot of money on raingear, I'd opt for a poncho. If I wanted more versatility, I'd get lightweight coated nylon rain pants and rain jacket. I'd make sure the hood was comfortable; I'd try to keep pockets to a minimum; I'd like to

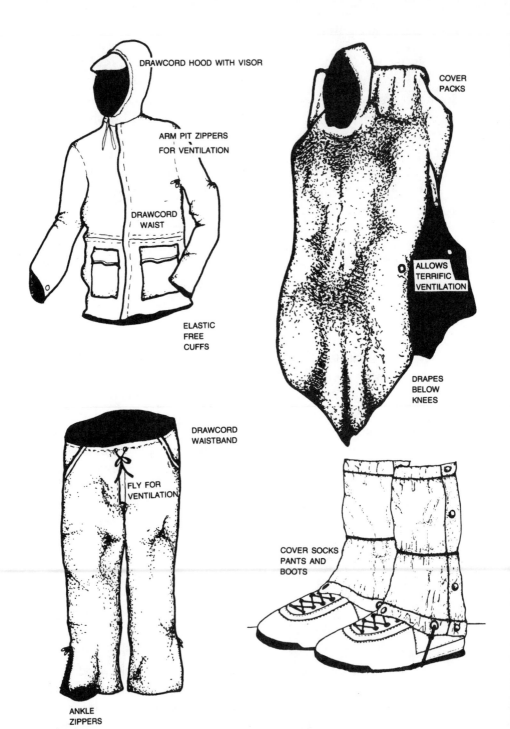

DRAWCORD HOOD WITH VISOR

COVER PACKS

ARM PIT ZIPPERS FOR VENTILATION

DRAWCORD WAIST

ALLOWS TERRIFIC VENTILATION

ELASTIC FREE CUFFS

DRAPES BELOW KNEES

DRAWCORD WAISTBAND

FLY FOR VENTILATION

COVER SOCKS PANTS AND BOOTS

ANKLE ZIPPERS

Figure 3   A poncho allows excellent ventilations, but limited protection. Gaiters offer protection for pants, socks, and boots. A well-made rain suit system will provide adequate ventilation. Look for a system with these important features.

see armpit zippers for extra ventilation; I'd prefer that the jacket didn't have elastic in the wrists, because elasticized wrists are difficult to ventilate; I'd prefer a drawcord waist and a fly front on the pants (ventilation again), and I'd like short zippers at the ankles so I could pull the pants on and off without taking my boots off. Would I look at one of the waterproof/breathable fabrics like Gore-Tex? Probably not, unless I was planning to do a lot of cool and cold-weather walking for long periods of time.

RAINGEAR COMPARISON

ADVANTAGES	DISADVANTAGES
NYLON	
Relatively inexpensive; practical for warm weather walks	Not breathable; traps perspiration inside saturating clothing; inexpensive might mean cheap; impractical for cold weather walks
GORETEX	
Breathable; allows perspiration to permeate through outer shell, clothes remain relatively dry; usually excellent construction; perfect for cool & cold weather	Relatively expensive; impractical for warm weather walks
PLASTIC/POLY	
Very inexpensive	Traps perspiration; not breathable; induces increased perspiration; practically disposable

Figure 4
Raingear comparison chart.

Warmwear. For most woods-walking, you can scrounge through your dresser and your closet. The summer foray rarely requires more than a light sweater held in reserve, and a pair of loose, comfortable shorts or pants. Please note that *"loose and comfortable"* does NOT include jeans or cut-off jeans, which are usually cut wrong for walking, and which soak up water like a sponge.

If you like things that are techy — and that just plain work!

— pick up a lightweight polypropylene underwear top and a lightweight fiberpile jacket or pullover of the type that's usually found with the paddling clothing. The combination of undershirt and pile is cozy in even quite cool weather, yet breathable enough to be a pleasant addition in the morning or at twilight on even a warm day. Hint: the polypro undershirt should have long sleeves; it's a bit of sun protection with essentially zero warmth when worn by itself. How did I find that out? On a two-week canoe trip (with a lot of ground exploration) in the Florida Everglades. Winter underwear in the subtropics!

Compass. You'll want one, even if you might not need one right away. Besides, a compass is even more fun than a good diamond whetstone as a time-waster. And who knows? You never can tell when you'll need a sharp knife or the esoteric map-and-compass skills you honed during lunch.

Get a compass with a transparent base plate, the kind you can lay on a map and use for real navigation. Forget the little round jobs with wiggly (induction-damped) needles, as they're less accurate and a pain to use. Ten bucks or so will get you a very reliable instrument that's capable of greater accuracy than you can use.

Personal Gear. This is another one of those wonderful catchall phrases that can cover everything from an 8 x 10 view camera to a few sheets of toilet paper. For a day's walk in the woods, take what you will need and what will enrich the jaunt. When you're carrying your whole house on your back, you have to be more ruthless with your whims, or you'll wind up toting forty pounds of lightweight, high-tech stuff you don't need.

What do I think is necessary for a random scoot in my nearby Huron National Forest? Sunglasses, insect repellent (which I very rarely use), toilet paper in a ziploc bag, a pocket knife, binoculars (mine are big old fat ones; I'd love a pair of the vest-pocket lightweights), a bird guide and wildflower guide, a small notebook and pen, and the Book of Common Prayer of the Episcopal Church. To me , a walk in the woods is a time for both external and internal exploration. You may be happier with a Frisbee and a harmonica. But — don't forget the bug dope, sunglasses and toilet paper!

Figure 5
A basic daypack with a very useful front pocket.

Figure 6
A basic daypack with a "suit-case" zipper allows for quick access to the contents.

Where To Put All This. In a pack, of course. But not the pack you'll be using for overnighting and longer trips. For day trips, you want a small pack that will comfortably hold everything you'll need, with a little extra capacity for winter jaunts.

Our family has grown up and flown the coop, taking most of their gear with them, so Molly and I range the local countryside by ourselves. We each have a small day pack and midsized rucksack from which to choose, and the most common pairing is one small pack each. In cooler weather, one of us will take the larger rucksack. In winter, we'll each take a large rucksack if we plan to have a hot mug-up for lunch.

When you go looking for small and midsized packs, you'll

face a bewildering variety of gear and wide price range. Keep these hints in mind as you look.

1.   Bells and whistles are only useful if they're bells you usually ring and whistles you usually blow.

2.   While a subframe is usually superfluous for a light pack, a thin foam pad built into the pack helps the pack keep its shape, helps it to carry better, and keeps the edges of your bird guide from excavating a hole in your back. It is NOT sissy to be comfortable. Just remember old Nessmuk's classic dictum from the turn of the century: *"We do not go into the woods to rough it. We go to smooth it. We get it rough enough in town."*

Figure 7
A teardrop shaped backpack provides more freedom of movement.

3.   Even the most slender waistband helps to keep the pack stabilized and keeps it from bouncing. You don't need to worry about magical phrases like *"transferring the weight to your hips"* when you're carrying eight pounds.

4.   Firmly padded shoulder straps are mandatory.

5.   Lots of cute little pockets and zippers look official, but are usually more trouble than they're worth. However, a teardrop pack that's divided into a top and bottom compartment is well worth the price, and a larger rucksack with either a header (the pocket on the flap), a front pocket, or side pockets (make sure they fit your water bottle — or buy water bottles to fit) is very handy to use.

6. The price of a pack reflects its materials and its sewing time (for which read *"complexity"*). By and large, you get what you pay for.

7. If you hike with kids, remember that they'll fuss if they carry a tiny pack — and they'll fuss more if they don't. Make them a part of the adventure rather than an onerous duty. If you walk with kids, get packs for the kids.

Strangely enough, probably the second most important piece of backpacking gear (after your head) is neither bedroom nor kitchen nor pack itself. It's what you wear on your feet — which is more than just a pair of boots. And if we didn't talk about boots when we were chatting about a day's walk in the woods, it's because casual walking with next to no equipment on your back can be done in casual footgear. Specialized terrain requires at least a look at more specialized shoes, and putting 20-25% of your weight on your back and *schlepping* it around up hill and down dale requires more than a look, unless you're young, strong, immune to pain, and plan to live forever. So ... let's look at boots. And at how to walk!

Boots. I've never liked the word *"hiking"* except as it dealt with sailboats, and *"backpacking"* has a macho sweatiness about it that grates on me. But *"boots"* has a solid, honest ring to it. There are *shoes;* they're made to look pretty and to protect my feet from dog droppings and broken glass. And these are *boots,* made to keep my feet comfortable and provide a solid working platform for me while I roam around in that wonderful country north of Highway 20. There's a difference.

Time was when boots were leather. Period. Time was when the very best backcountry boots (as opposed to mountaineering boots) were made of either full hide roughout or smoothout leather, oiltanned, stitched to an 8-iron leather midsole, with another 8-iron midsole doubler and a 10-iron rubber filler. The union of the mid-soles and uppers would be effected with a Norwegian welt, and the outsole would be a heavy-duty black Vibram lug. The resulting boots weighed maybe 5 pounds per pair, took forever to break in, required maintenance, and were nearly indestructible if you had the sense God gave a goose. That was then. In 1968, boots built like that could be had for under $60 a pair. Today? Don't ask.

Figure 8   Lightweight, flexible boots allow freedom of movement and balance. With the recent athletic shoe design and a good fit, you will feel like you're walking on air, instead of 50 tons.

But this might not be all bad. I think we made too much of a fetish of the Superboot back then. We all wanted to be heroes; we all wanted to look like we were departing for the North Wall of the Eiger tomorrow. Lightweight boots were bought by women, children and birdwatchers. Real Men, by God, wore Real Boots!

I still have a pair of Real Boots, bench made by the French firm of Galibier. They're masterpieces. And unless I was going on a snow or mixed snow and ice climb where I needed crampons, you wouldn't ever find me wearing them. They're just too much boot!

Hear this. If the criteria for real estate is *"Location, location and location,"* the criteria for backpacking footgear is *"Fit, fit and fit."* Yes, your footgear should be sufficiently sturdy as to hold together throughout a trip. Yes, it should provide protection for your feet. Yes, it should provide a firm foundation for walking and scrambling. BUT ...

No, it need not be bombproof. No, it need not last forever. No, it need not be *"waterproof."*

Good grief! Uncle Harry Roberts, the Last of the Old-Time Tech Warriors, advocating what amounts to *"throw-away"* boots?

Yeah. Sort of. The last few years have seen a genuine revolution in backcountry footgear. The new boots, derived from athletic shoe technology and essentially untouched by human hands in manufacture, are light, comfortable right out of the box, engineered by some person who has made computer studies of what happens to feet when their owner is toting a pack up a hill, and functional. Do they last forever? Who cares?

Let me expand on that idea a bit. The only activities I can think of where the durability of a piece of equipment is often considered to be more important than the functionality of the equipment are backpacking and canoeing. I'm constantly mystified at this. I'm even more mystified at the collateral notion that *"performance"* is a dirty word, right up there with *"stylish"* in the lexicon of the average woodchuck. Thank you, I'll carry the very light tent, even if it requires more care and even if it won't withstand a summit gale on Rainier. Thank you, I'll paddle the quick canoe that weighs under 50 pounds, even if it might be a hair less rugged than a plastic bruisewater. Thank you, I'll ski on the very lightest touring skis that meet my needs rather than on some flattened water rollers that will withstand collision with a tree. Why? Because the gear that's light, responsive and designed to perform is simply a lot more fun to use. It may take a little more skill — or even a lot more skill — to learn to pitch the tent in the sheltered area, or miss the rocks with the canoe (yes, you can miss the rocks!), or miss the tree on your skis. But you spend your life doing skill-oriented things — unless you regularly stop your automobile by bouncing it off the end of your garage!

Get the neat stuff, the light stuff, the fun stuff, and learn to use it. That way, you'll return again and again to the outback, and you'll enjoy it more each time. Get the clunky stuff, and you won't enjoy it — unless you're into flagellation.

Footgear As A Total Concept. The boot is only a part of the picture. Generally, when you buy a pair of boots — or shoes of any sort — you try them on with socks of the sort that you plan to wear with them. Otherwise, the shoe doesn't fit well. The socks, then, are a part of the whole package of protection for your feet. Unless you hike regularly in hot, damp conditions, consider wearing one pair of fairly heavy socks (I prefer a stretch ragg wool) and one pair of light liner socks (again, wool is my preference) next to your skin. Why the dual sock package? The contemporary lightweight boot flexes nicely and breaks in easily, but none of us are very compulsive about keeping our boots laced properly, so they fit snugly but comfortably and don't shift on our feet as we walk. So the boots slop around. If you're wearing one sock, the boot and the outer sock tend to move as a unit, and scrub against your heel and the top of your toes at the metatarsal heads. If you're wearing a lightweight liner sock, it will tend to hang on to your foot. As the boot moves, the socks rub against each other. And I don't care if my *socks* get blisters!

But footgear encompasses more than boots and socks. If the trend in contemporary bootmaking is toward lightweight boots, which may be somewhat less protective and *"waterproof"* than boots of the past, it behooves you to look for sneaky little ways to increase protection without greatly increasing weight. (Remember that old saw about *"one pound on your feet is like five pounds on your back"*? You do? Take it to the bank. It's sure.) Let's look at a piece of gear that was very popular with both backpackers and ski tourers in the past — ironically, when boots were heavier. It's called the gaiter. It's nothing more than a tube of coated nylon with a zipper up the side, and a cord that goes under the bootsole. It covers the top of your boot, and excludes rain, ticks, sand, pebbles and other things that make walking a chore. Gaiters — low-cut ones for three-season travel — are simply worth their weight in gold. Don't leave home without them.

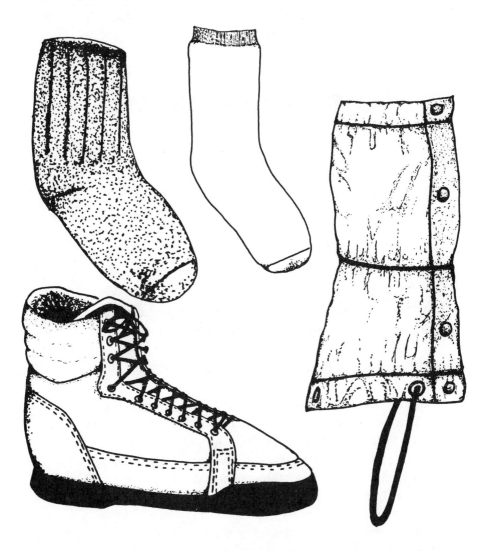

Figure 9 Footgear as a total concept includes thin inner liner socks (polypropyleneor wool), flexible boots, a thick outer sock (stretch ragg wool) and gaiters to keep the snow or rain from your feet.

4. THE HOUSE YOU LIVE IN

The house you live in on the trail is a system, made up of tent, tarp, groundcloth, sleeping pad and sleeping bag.

Before we get into a discussion about gear and its use, let me preface this whole bag of worms with one simple statement and one simple conclusion.

The statement is this:

The house you live in is the heaviest part of your gear. And the conclusion inevitably follows, as night must follow day:

The less your house weighs, the easier it will be to carry.

Admit it. Were you really surprised?

The Tent. Unless you plan to hike with the family, you'll be looking at a small two-person tent. It may be a double A-frame, with poles fore and aft in the form of an A. It may have an A-frame pole setup in the front and a single pole in the rear. It may be a modified dome. Unless you're planning on camping on the Catenary Ridge of Mt. Logan or some equally insane spot, you're not interested in a tent's ability to stand up to 60-knot winds.

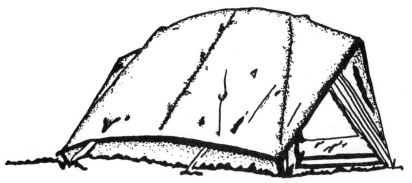

Figure 10   A popular self-supporting double A-Frame with ridgepole. A bit heavy, perhaps, but well-designed, roomy, stable and convenient.

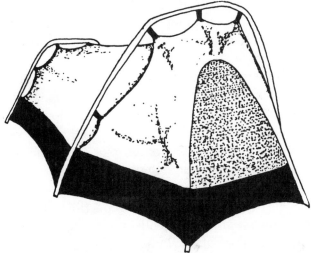

Figure 11   A small double-hoop design offers both stability and head room, however, has little floor space.

Figure 12   The dome tent is easy to erect, free-standing and roomy, but is heavy. However, top-of-the-line aluminum poles can reduce the weight by over a third, at a cost increase of about 20%.

Let me digress about winds. I live in one of the few wooded spots in the country where wind power generation is feasible and economically sound. The typical day is 10 to 20 knot winds. In Autumn, what Gordon Lightfoot called *"the gales of November,"* and which may run from October through December, are a fact of life. I can remember one day of winds in excess of 60 knots up here on the shores of Lake Huron. Don't go blithely talking about 60 knot winds — or listening to people talking about them with absolute credulity — until you've seen one. The chance of experiencing one on a valley floor in wooded country is so remote as to be effectively out of the question.

In short, then, three things really dictate your choice — space, weight and convenience. They're all interrelated, but we can look at them separately.

Space is largely self-explanatory. Just keep in mind that space considerations are three-dimensional. For example: my wife and I aren't as slim as we once were, but we're still long, stringy people who can coexist in a narrow tent quite well. However, we need more headroom than would a shorter pair, and we'll sacrifice tent width for tent height and tent length, unless the height and length add too much weight. Space is also a function of ventilation. A small tent with large screens and a good flow of air is felt to be more roomy than a larger tent with small vent space. Also, a dark tent is perceived as smaller. Some people like to feel that the tent is small. It becomes, for them, a safe, snug, dry cave. Others need room. How do you find out what you prefer? Go to your outfitter's and climb into the tents in which you're interested. And if you hike with your spouse, bring your spouse. Both have to agree on the desirability of the tent. And do me two favors, please. Don't become a tech-weenie. Guys are prone to play this game on their mates due to some warped idea of what constitutes self-enhancement. Don't play the stitches-per-inch game, particularly if you're doing it to offset what you think of as a *"whim"* — like the fact that she thinks Tent A is more comfortable and pleasant than Tent B, and you think that Tent B is simply neat as hell and techy. Hey — take the tent the lady will use. Save the techy stuff for a Great Equipment Shootout at Dead Hiker Clearing.

Weight is so important that it must be considered with every piece of gear. We've already established that the tent needn't be

TENTS	Seasons	Sleeping Capacity	Floor Area (sq.ft.)	Average Weight	Price
EUREKA GOSSAMER	3	1	21.28	2 lbs. 14 oz.	A
EUREKA TIMBERLINE 2	3	2	37.63	6 lbs. 15 oz.	A
KELTY GEMINI	3	2	36.25	4 lbs. 13 oz.	B
MOSS STARLET II	3	2	29	4 lbs. 12 oz.	E
SIERRA DESIGNS DIVINE LIGHT	3	1	20	2 lbs. 3 oz.	C
NORTHFACE DRAGONFLY	3	2	47	5 lbs. 6 oz.	E

Figure 13   A chart of popular backpacking tents.

Famous brand tents offer an interest-
ing assortment for backpackers.
Remember that space considerations
are three dimensional. Height,
width and length are very important.

Price Range

A   0 - 99
B 100 - 149
C 150 - 199
D 200 - 249
E 250 - 349
F 350 - 500

bombproof, because you're not camping on exposed ridges, and you're an adult who takes care of your toys. Indestructibility is way down your priority list. Consider also that you may well carry a groundcloth if it looks like you're in for a possible heavy rain, and you will carry a small, lightweight tarp to use as a cooking fly and a *"vestibule"* for your tent. I know. Hard people cook in a rain and like it. I *can* cook in a rain, but I'd as soon cook under a tarp when it's raining, thank you. It's so much kinder to things like coffee, sugar and people!

If you use a tarp, this may augment the size of the tent to where you can live with a smaller one, which will probably weigh less. Most tents are made of fabric that weighs about 2 ounces per yard, whether or not it's coated. Netting weighs less, but not as much less as you'd think. The equation is simple. The larger the tent, the more fabric it takes to make it, and the more pole sections it takes to support it. You can, with some tents, choose Easton arrow shaft stock pole sets (impeccable!) as an option, and save a pound or more. Bring money. It's a worthwhile trade. *"Well, it weighs five pounds more, but it saved me $80"* is small consolation halfway up Blister Butte in a rainstorm.

What's an acceptable weight for a two-person tent that will turn weather away and be more than a portable doghouse? I'd like to think about 5½ pounds all up — tent, fly, pole set, stakes and stuff bag.

Convenience is something only you can determine. And you can only determine it by setting the tent up a few times at your outfitter's. If something deep down inside tells you that you'll never adapt to that nifty storm closure at three in the morning when the rain starts and you're still foggy from sleep, don't get the tent! If it takes forever to set up, or needs four different pole sets, all of which differ by an inch in length and you can't tell one from the other until they're all in place, don't get the tent. I don't care how neat looking it is, if you wouldn't want to set it up in a hard rain, don't get the tent!

Get it?

Erecting Your House. Remember what all the books on camping and backpacking told you about where to pitch your tent? Here's a specimen, in case you missed all that schlog — or in case you're in need of a belly laugh to get through the day.

"Seek out a spot that's high and dry, grassy but not boggy, facing the East so the morning sun will cheer you, and shaded, but not under trees that might blow over on you in a storm, or draw lightning to you. Further, the site should be close to potable water and should have copious firewood nearly."

There may be ten such spots in the continental United States that aren't for sale for $2743 a square foot. There are maybe forty such in Canada — but that's the good news. The bad news is that you have to walk 186 miles to get to all of them, and most of them require the ascent and descent of 12,000 foot ice walls.

Where, in these days of crowded trails and densely-packed designated camping areas in the backcountry, do you make your home? *Anywhere you can find a flat spot, friend!*

This is the problem. We've exceeded the carrying power of the range, as it were. We all want the magical experience; we all head to the legendary places to walk, just as we all head to the legendary places to paddle and to ski. And these places are neat. No doubt! That's why they became legends in the first place. But keep in mind that the legendary places usually had the benefit of either good press-agentry or were proximate to a major metropolitan area, or both. This certainly helped both the White Mountains and the Adirondacks, and some of the prime Western areas have been puffed up by the media as well. Meanwhile, I can start from my front door and walk across the upper part of Michigan's Lower Peninsula on a wonderful trail that courses through the jackpine, sand and bog ecology of the Huron and Manistee National Forests, and have the place to myself. That's where two of those ten campsites are, in fact!

Don't get me wrong. A walk through the jackpines in Michigan is not the same experience as a walk through Indian Henry's Hunting Ground on the Wonderland Trail, with Mt. Rainier looming over your shoulder to the Northeast and the valley of Tahoma Creek and Emerald Ridge in your face. In fact, I'm not sure that anywhere on earth comes up to the Wonderland as a constantly varied scenic experience. But spectacular scenery isn't the only reason we walk. There are no sweeping vistas on the Shore-to-Shore Trail in Michigan. But the bird life is profuse and varied, the biosphere (boreal forest) varies with twenty feet of elevation gain and loss, and while it's mostly jackpine, you begin to gain an appreciation for good old *Pinus banksiana* as a forest tree. It may be a junk tree in some places, but up here, halfway between the Equator and the North Pole, it's what grows, and you learn to love it. There are quiet places in the world where you learn to look in deep rather than out far. My Michigan is one of them. So are the Georgia coast and the Everglades.

So, in all probability, is the country around where you live. Get to know it, and you most likely can find a level, breezy, dry campsite that's close to potable water — or close to water, at any rate. Don't pass up a trip to the great places, ever. But don't ever define them as the only places where backpacking exists. Because it exists everywhere. And it's good everywhere.

Okay. So we might not find the perfect place to pitch a tent. What can we do about it?

A fair amount, actually, particularly if you keep in mind that the tent and tarp are simply shelter for the night, not a permanent abode. If you're setting up the tent as a base camp for day hikes, you may want to scrounge for a quality site, because you may want to spend a day hanging out at base camp, reading and renewing yourself. On the other hand, you could always move you and your book and your sleeping pad a quarter-mile to a neat flat rock in the sun with little effort.

Try for the ideal site, obviously. Of all the criteria, I'd choose *"smooth and level"* above all if it didn't look like rain, and *"high and dry"* if it did. However, there isn't much I can do about *"smooth and level"* if the site isn't that way to begin with, assuming that I'm smart enough to remove loose stones and sticks, but there is something I can do about keeping relatively dry in a relatively wet campsite.

Several things, in fact.

First, make sure you've sealed all the seams exposed to rain, windblown rain and groundwater in both the tent and the flysheet. This isn't an onerous job. Pick a rain-free day, set up the tent, and do it. Take your time. Fuss over it. Enjoy the rapport with Old Buddy Tent.

In all honesty, seam sealing isn't 100% effective. But it helps; it gives you an edge, as it were, and it is certainly something that's within your power to control.

Check that notion out for a paragraph. *"Within your power to control;"*; wow! There are a lot of things that are within your power to control if you focus your gaze in close rather than far out. You cannot redesign the tent — but you can jiggle it and wiggle it to where it works. You cannot stop the Pollution Of The Oceans — but you can do a helluva job of stopping the Local Megaslob from dumping crap into the Local River, or stopping the Local Bandit from turning parkland into Dee — Velopment. If you focus on the big picture, you'll live frustrated and die unhappy. But if you take care of what you can take care of, you'll do just fine. Start by sealing the seams of your tent.

That you do at home. This you do at home and in the field. If it looks like a rainy weekend, or if you're going out for a longer trip, or if you're the belt-and-suspenders type, tote with you either a piece of 4-mil plastic that's a few inches larger in all dimensions than your tent floor, or tote a piece of coated nylon taffeta — the lightweight stuff, 2 ounce per yard nominal — of similar dimensions, and use that as a ground cloth. But ... a ground cloth with a difference! *This* ground cloth doesn't go on the ground! It goes *inside* the tent! Why? Because water can't sneak between the tent floor and the ground cloth when the ground cloth is inside. It can otherwise, and it will be driven through the tent floor and into your bedroom. *"Ground"* cloth inside, then. Just like a rug. OK?

The third thing is *all* field work. All you have to do at home is remember to bring the tarp with you, and the parachute cord with which to rig it.

Lightweight coated nylon tarps are wonderful things. They enable you to cook and lounge in comfort during a downpour; they shield your stove from wind; they create a feeling of companionship around a small fire at night; they're neat.

They're neater if you rig them right. Get the kind with grommets rather than funny little tie-tapes, and rig the grommets with little loops of lightweight shock cord. This keeps the tarp alive when the wind gets busy.

Generally, I prefer to erect the tarp in such a way that it shields the tent entrance. (In fact, it's not at all inappropriate to rig the tarp before you set up the tent, if it's raining. If the tarp is kept where it's easily accessible, you and your pack can live in relative comfort while you set up the tent.) Run the pitch of the tarp away from the tent, please, so it if does rain, you don't funnel the runoff onto the tent. Make sure you have headroom. And enjoy the dry feeling when the rain starts. You even have somewhere to take off your raingear before you get into the snug, dry tent! Isn't that great?

Hint: Keep the tarp in its own stuff bag, and keep the chute cord you use to rig it, neatly coiled, with it. This both keeps a potentially wet piece of gear isolated in the pack, and it ensures that you'll be able to find what you need to rig the thing next night, even if it's dark and rainy.

And that's about all you need to know about setting up tents. *About* all. If you have a new tent, it helps to practice setting it up once or twice before you have to set it up in the dark, and it helps old hands to unpack their Old Buddy Tent before they leave, set it up, and check for things that may have been lost or misplaced from the last trip. Yes, I have left my little stake bag at home! That's not a total loss; stakes can be readily fashioned. But the fancy aluminum pole sets for a dome tent can't be. Leave those puppies at home and you have a problem!

Sleeping Bags and Pads. In the past, this would have been the time for a learned disquisition on the internal structure of down sleeping bags, and a solemn, sententious treatise on the differences between down and synthetic insulation.

I don't think we need to go through that again — ever. The choices are simple. So are the tradeoffs. Down is lighter per unit thickness. It is more compressible, which means it fits into a smaller stuff bag than would a synthetic bag of the same size and thickness. It is more sensitive to atmospheric moisture and insensible perspiration than synthetic fill, but you can completely discard the old notion that *"you can't sleep in a wet down bag, but you can in a wet synthetic bag."* You can't sleep in either one! However, you can dry the synthetic bag in the field. But — how in the world did you get your sleeping bag that wet anyway?

I get this from canoeists all the time. *"Well, I use synthetic insulation, so when I tip over, it'll ..."* What do you mean, *when* you tip over, klutz? The backpacker's analogy is *"when I fall off the log that crosses the stream."* I've heard that, too.

Consider this. If your sleeping bag is stuffed in its little nylon house called a stuff bag, and is inside your pack, it's tough to get it wet. In fact, take a down bag well stuffed and try to get it wet by immersing it in a sink filled with water. You'll wet a little at the mouth of the stuff sack, and that's all. All of which means that if you've gotten your sleeping bag truly thoroughly wet, you probably managed to do that by leaving it out on a flat rock to air out and left it there during a hard rain. At that point, sleep in your pile jacket, lightweight long johns and stocking cap with your feet stuffed into your pack, and consider that a benign deity chose to merely inconvenience you for your stupidity rather than killing you like you deserved.

Given a choice of bags, I'd choose a mummy in the 20-30 degree range, and what with the development of highly compressible synthetic insulations, it might well be a synthetic bag. Knowing my taste for neat stuff, though, and my general desire to go light, I might choose a down-filled mummy in the same comfort range.

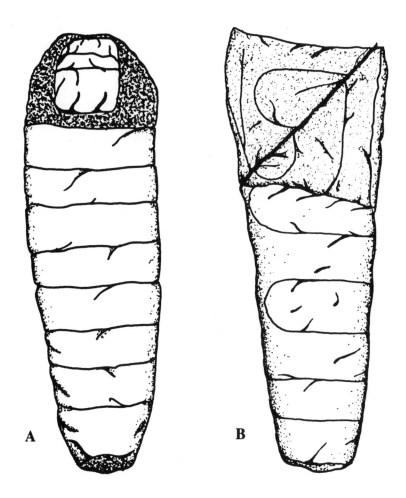

Figure 14   (A) The mummy style sleeping bag has been noted to have the "most efficient shape."

(B) Many people prefer the comfort of the modified square-cut bag, particularly in summer.

Sleep Pads and Mattresses	Constr.	Dimensions	Weight	Price
Therm-a-Rest Mat™, Regular	D	1½" x 20" x 48"	1lb. 8oz.	C
Therm-a-Rest Mat™, Long	D	1½" x 20" x 72"	2lb. 5oz.	C
Ultra Light T-Rest™, Regular	D	1" x 20" x 47"	1lb. 1oz.	C
Ultra Light T-Rest™, Long	D	1" x 20" x 72"	1lb. 12oz.	C
T-Rest Camp Rest™	D	2" x 25" x 77"	3lb. 5½oz.	D
Common Air Mat, Regular	C	2½" x 28" x 60"	1lb. 8oz.	B
Common Air Mat, Long	C	2½" x 28" x 72"	1lb. 10oz.	B
Ridge Rest™, Regular	A	⅝" x 20" x 48"	9oz.	B
Ridge Rest™, Long	A	⅝" x 20" x 72"	14oz.	B
Nylon-Covered Foam Pad, Regular	B	1½" x 20" x 50"	1lb. 11oz.	B
Nylon-Covered Foam Pad, Long	B	1½" x 20" x 72"	2lb. 7oz.	B
Common Closed Cell Pad, Regular	A	⅜" x 22" x 56"	9oz.	A
Common Closed Cell Pad, Long	A	⅜" x 22" x 70"	11oz.	A

Construction

A = Closed cell foam usually
EVA closed cell foam

B = Open cell foam usually
polyurethane foam

C = Air

D = Air and open celled
foam combination

Price Rating Equivalency

A = 0 - 9

B = 10 - 24

C = 25 - 49

D = 50 - 99

Figure 15   A chart of popular sleeping pads and mattresses.

Now, *"comfort range"* is another weasel phrase. There are times when I'm comfortable at 10 degrees in a *"30 degree"* bag, and there are times when nothing short of a waterbed with the temperature cranked up to *"womb"* will do.

You see, sleeping comfortably depends on skill, in the long run. It depends on how well you manage your caloric intake and your fluid intake, for one. Try to *"walk off some suet"* in the outback, and you'll probably be chilly. Go without fluid on a cool day when you don't feel thirsty and walk off 3% of your body weight (that's only 4.5 pounds for a 150-pounder!), and you'll be chilly. Walk off 5% of your body weight and you might become a medical emergency in a big hurry.

Hang around the campfire in damp, sweaty clothing and you'll sleep cold. Wear damp clothing in your sleeping bag and you'll sleep cold. Put your sleeping bag on the ground — tent floor and groundcloth don't count for warmth — and you'll sleep cold. Wind down the day with three good jolts of 100 proof *"to warm you up"* and you'll sleep cold. Smoke and you'll sleep cold.

And chances are you'll blame the sleeping bag!

How to sleep warm? Use a foam sleeping pad or a foam pad that can be inflated for extra comfort (it's called a Therm-A-Rest, and it's as much a part of my overnighting gear as my head). That buys you quite a few degrees of comfort. Eat regularly and lightly; don't stuff yourself and hit the sack. Maintain a proper fluid balance. Drink water — and don't mix it half and half with Mr. Jack. Wear dry underclothing (or nothing at all) in your sleeping bag. If you wake up chilly, a mouthful of water sometimes helps. So might a mouthful of trail mix — but don't keep that in the tent, please. A bear next to you would keep you plenty warm, but not in a way you'd really like. And — wear a hat! I take a funky old red woolen watch cap with me even on canoeing trips in Florida. This hat has been with me on some winter climbs in rough situations and on casual overnights with my kids on the *"back mountain."* Mostly it stays in my pack. But when I'm tired and it's chilly, it goes on, probably as early as when we make camp. The key to staying warm is to stay warm; don't get chilled in the first place. It's a lot harder to *regain* warmth than to *retain* warmth.

So ... don't keep your shirt on. Keep your hat on.

5. THE KITCHEN

We haven't talked much about food and the means of preparing it. It isn't easy to talk about food, except in generalizations, because some folks will build four-course meals over an open fire, and whip up blueberry muffins for breakfast, while others would just as soon brew up that grim concoction known as freeze-dried veggie beef stew and woof it down with neither joy nor enlightenment. I prefer to scrounge leftovers, myself, and bring nothing but Christian Brothers brandy and good coffee, and trade that for food. However, that doesn't always work, so I subsist nicely in that gray area between Campfire Cordon Bleu and Gutbomb Veggie Beef Stew.

I do have a couple of rules that I mostly follow.

Rule One is the Lazy Person's Rule. Never cook anything that takes more than one pot unless it's a layover day — and somebody else brought the extra pot.

Rule Two is the Hungry Person's Rule. Never cook anything that takes much more than fifteen minutes from pack to stomach.

Rule Three is the Contemplative Person's Rule. Before you unpack, before you even make camp, brew up a cup of soup or a cup of coffee, sprawl out on your Therm-A-Rest, and enjoy, enjoy.

The only time to violate this rule is when it's raining, in which case you set up your tarp and *then* brew up the cup of comfort. Under those conditions, it's acceptable to opt for coffee and brandy, provided you share it.

Rule Four is the Thoughtful Person's Rule. Cooking is done over a camp stove. Campfire cooking is for absolute emergencies, or for areas where there's so much dead and down wood that you might just as well use it. The joker there is that such areas are prime fire hazards. Play it right and you could burn down half of Saskatchewan.

Fortunately, the decision is usually taken from you. Many popular hiking areas prohibit fires, period. And in many others, the dead-and-down wood has been scrounged for a square mile around by three generations of romantics.

Don't misunderstand me. I like a small campfire, and where it's ecologically sane to build one, I will. There's something primordial about a campfire. You almost can see the eyes gleaming in the night at the edge of the fire's glow, and somewhere just beyond your hearing is the throaty rumble of a big cat. A romantic notion, perhaps. But I don't think many of us are immune to that kind of romance. I'm not, for sure.

Camp Stoves. But campfires are not cooking fires. Food is cooked over a camp stove, a one-burner job that may be fueled by gasoline (more accurately, Coleman fuel), kerosene (rarely), butane or propane (very convenient but not very *"hot,"* or alcohol (commonly found in wonderfully-made nesting European cooksets, of which the Trangia label is the *piece de resistance*). I use a butane stove a lot in summer. I recognize its limitation. It's bulky; the fuel cartridge can't be removed until all the fuel is used, so you can't change out just before a trip even though you know that the cartridge on the stove won't last; it's less than efficient in a wind, and you have *"empties"* to schlepp back out. On the plus side, the little stove throttles down beautifully, lights instantly, the cartridges can be changed out faster than I can fill a gasoline-fired stove. I don't have the potential fire hazard of volatile liquid around, and I don't have to worry about the possibility of fuel leaking into the pack.

Use whatever best suits your temperament. There are times when I'm so relaxed that the quiet little butane stove, and its unhurried cooking pace, is just what I want. Other times, I want to torch off my gasoline stove, boil the living hell out of something FAST, and eat. I suspect you're the same. Neither of us wants to carry two stoves on a trip. So we settle for one, and we're wrong half the time. And it doesn't really matter. If I had to settle for one stove only, it would be a small pressurized gasoline stove like the Coleman Peak 1. And I would learn how to maintain it — and I'd maintain it before it needed maintenance. The time to diddle with a small stove is during the week, and the place is at home.

Stoves	Fuel	Weight (oz.) Without Fuel	Price
Optimus 199 Ranger	ABC	31.4	C
MSR Whisper Lite	B	13.3	B
MSR X-Gk	AB	18.8	D
Coleman Peak 1 - Multi Fuel	ABC	18.6	C
Coleman Peak 1	B	29.2	B
SVEA 123R	B	18.2	B
GAZ C206 Bleuet	E	11.6	A

Fuel	Fuel Price
A = Kerosene	A = 0 - 24
B = White Gas	B = 25 - 49
C = Alcohol	C = 50 - 74
D = Gasoline (leaded, no lead, aviation)	D = 75 - 100
E = Butane	

Figure 16   When considering fuel type, pay attention to differences in boiling time per pint of fuel required to boil a quart of water. Remember to carry a carefully waterproofed set of matches or a lighter. Consider fuel container weight not included above.

Food. Eat what you like, but don't spare the carbohydrates. That's what you run on.

Some hints. Most food — especially grocery store stuff —

must be repackaged for easy stowage. Also, there's no point in bringing a whole jar of instant coffee on an overnight when all you'll need is a few teaspoonsful. If you don't need it, don't bring it. It's that simple. However, I've always brought a few extras, specifically a few extra bags of Success Rice (wondeful stuff!) and a couple packages of soup mix. Stuff the rice and the soup mix in a heavy-duty ziploc bag, and forget it until you absolutely need it, or you feel like a very bland change of pace.

There's a lesson here. If you divide the world up into belly fillers like rice, pasta and instant mashed potatoes, protein sources like freeze-dried meats, sauces like soup mixes and gravy mixes, and veggies like, well, veggies, you can sort of pick one from each column, throw them into the pot, and go for it. This isn't my system. It was created by June Fleming, who wrote for me back when I edited *Wilderness Camping* in the '70s, and who put it all into a book called *The Well-Fed Backpacker*, which was — and is — an absolute jewel of a no-nonsense how-to with a goodly touch of wit, and the best thing ever on trail cooking. She calls this system "One-Liners," and she has six categories, which can be combined into over *700,000* different meals, which should be more than enough to satisfy even the most jaded appetite.

Here are some things I do that makes cooking easier. Give 'em a try.

If I know I have to hydrate something recalcitrant for dinner, I put it into a wide-mouthed plastic jar, with water, and tote it in my pack for the day, or for the afternoon. This can almost make the Dreaded Veggie Beef Stew palatable.

The backcountry is not the place to get casual about cleanup of cookware. If you're only using one pot for cooking, and very likely eating out of that pot, take the time to do a good, thorough cleanup of that pot. And not in the creek, please. What I do is torch off a teapotful of water while I'm eating. This gives me hot water for coffee, and a reserve for pot-washing. And it somehow makes the whole operation painless, if you know what I mean.

Small screw-top plastic or metal containers are worth their weight. Check the cookgear shelves at your outfitters. Friction lids are questionable, in general, but I've used the Rubbermaid storage bowls that you find in any supermarket for some time now, and they're excellent.

There is little use for a frypan on the trail unless you plan to fish a lot. Otherwise, save the weight and leave it at home, unless it forms the cover of your cookset and you want it on to keep the nesting teapot, the cutlery, the potlifter and the cleanup material from migrating. Of course, you can do all that with a stuff sack, which is lighter and which keeps your pack clean. If you must take a frypan, get a coated one for easy cleanup, and get one with deep sides, so you can use it as a shallow pot.

If you use a stove that's gasoline-fire, keep the stove, the fuel bottle, and the little funnel you use to refill the stove in an outside pocket of the pack. Don't — please! — stow them inside.

The Ultimate Simplicity Cookset for two people is one small stove, one 1½ quart pot, one nesting teapot (or 1 quart pot), two large cups, two tablespoons, one 1 quart widemouthed polybottle, a few small plastic vials containing some spices (Oregano! Yeah!), and (if you can find one) a tiny ladle with a detachable handle. They come from France and they're wonderful. But that's for formal service. My wife and I simply eat out of the same pot most of the time. Add a "tea egg" if you're a tea drinker, and that's it.

Keep meals in proper perspective. Don't go hungry — but don't get bent out of shape if you're not serving gourmet food. You're not out there to cook.

Pray for the return of retort-pouch foods to the marketplace. Oh, how I looked forward to a toss-it-in-the-boiling-water treat of sweet and sour pork or shrimp Creole over a bed of Success Rice cooked in the same pot at the same time! Great chow, that. Took about fives minutes to prepare, and the taste was excellent. I know. Why carry water mixed with food when you have water out there? For convenience on a weekend is the answer. On a long trip, the extra weight would be distinctly burdensome. But for two days you can afford to live a little.

Remember, always, that you came out here to smell the flowers. While you're at it, enjoy the smell of your first cup of coffee in the morning, too, and the taste of your patented Rice Peculiar. The answer to *"Are we having fun yet?"* should be *"Yes!"*

6. CONTAINER FOR THINGS CONTAINED

Now, why in the world we wait until nearly the end of a book on backpacking to talk about the backpack? I mean, isn't that the most important part of your gear?

Well ... no. The most important part of your gear is what you carry in your head. One kilogram of wisdom and one gram of acceptance is worth tons of superlight, high-tech *stuff*.

Your pack is important, though. But it's neither more nor less important than any other piece of gear on which you depend, and considerably less important than the fit of your boots.

If you were to listen to some outfitters talk, or sit in on a Great Equipment Shootout at a camping area, you'd think that packs are right up there in complexity with things like F-15's, the human reproductive system, and great wine. C'mon, folks; let's be real. The human race has toted things on its collective back for millenia. There aren't that many secrets any more!

But the few secrets are worth knowing.

And the first secret is the same one we talked about with boots. *"Fit, fit and fit"* is the key to a comfortable pack. I wish I could give you some magic formula to insure that your next pack — be it a frame pack or a soft pack or a soft pack with an internal frame — will fit you perfectly. But I can't. Every pack out there might fit you just a bit differently and still work well. For example, I own two frame packs of rather different design. One is the straightforward ladder frame with a padded hipbelt, and the other is a complex hip-rider that kind of wraps around you and snuggles up to you. Both work well for me — and if I stand sideways to you, the angle the shoulder straps make with relationship to the long axis of my body is radically different from one pack to the other. The big soft packs in the family mostly all fit the same because, with one exception, they came from the same manufacturer, and are size variations on the same basic design.

How do you test for fit and comfort if you're buying a pack?

Start by letting the outfitter fit the pack to you. The pack should be loaded with a weight approximating 20% of your body weight, which is the maximum you should carry if you plan to enjoy your time in the outback. Less is better; less is more. When you try on the pack, wear a soft, simple belt, please. You can't carry a pack comfortably wearing a wide, stiff belt and a belt buckle that looks like you won the all-round cowboy award at the Fort Worth Fat Stock Show. If need be, make your own belt. Two D-rings and a length of climbing webbing will do the job.

The pack must be comfortable. The frame, that is, must be comfortable. It must fit well, allow you reasonable freedom of movement, not cramp your arms or compress your chest, and it must stay put when you walk. A pack that sways and meanders as you move is a pain in the neck until you get tired; then it becomes a hazard. At this point, the bag — the container for the things contained — is very nearly meaningless. The pack must fit. Period.

If I were pressed to choose one type of backpack for the beginning backpacker, I'd choose a packframe with a full wraparound hipbelt, and a packbag, divided top and bottom, that covers about 3/4 of the length of the frame, so I have the option of carrying gear underneath it. I'd also like a top extension on the packframe, so I could carry gear lashed to that if I chose.

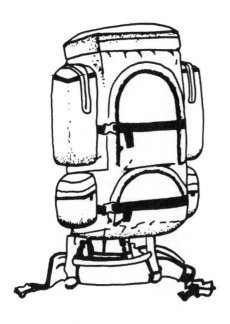

Figure 17
A pack with two main compartments and fair side pockets. The design transfers the weight of the pack to the hips.

What? No contemporary internal-frame pack?

No. Not now. The internal-frame pack is limited in terms of load distribution ability, and to a great extent is designed for people who have determined their gear over the years, and who use the internal-framed pack for specialty subsets within the sport. The relatively compact internal-frame bags are generally cut to permit considerable freedom of movement, so they're excellent for ski touring, bushwhacking, scrambling over rocks and anything else requiring flexible strength. For straight-ahead backpacking, though, I still think that most people are better suited by the frame pack.

Figure 18
Two different versions of day packs. Each are very popular.

A note in passing. We're enamored, as a nation, with multipurpose gadgets. (Is there any other way to explain a Vegamatic?) *"Hey, folkums, check it out! This pack is just perfect for backpacking, ski touring, rock climbing, canoeing and taking your three-month old to the supermarket so she can set a new world record by breaking 37 jars of Vlasic Polish dill pickles in one sweep of her chubby little fist! Hurry, hurry! Check it out!"*

Don't get trampled in the rush. There is no such thing as an all-purpose pack. If you canoe a lot, get a bespoke canoe pack. If you camp on skis, get a pack designed for the job. Otherwise, you'll go through five *"all-purpose"* Vegamatics — oops, sorry, packs — before you give up in disgust and do it the right way, which is to have a pack for a function or for a closely-related group of functions.

Hints On Packing. You're best served if you keep the heavier items high in the pack and close to the back of the pack — the part which lies against the frame.

Here's how I do it. The tent, and the tarp, both go on top of the pack, lashed to the extension bar. The sleeping bag/sleeping pad, also in its stuff bag, goes on the frame under the pack bag. If I had a full-length bag (which I don't like much), the sleeping gear would go into the big bottom compartment. As my packbag is divided, food and cookgear would go in the top compartment, resting on top of whatever I chose to take along for warmth. That's usually a lightweight polypro shirt, polypro long johns (even in summer!), and a lightweight pile jacket. This area catches any extra clothing I might bring, too, such as a change of undershorts and socks. The stove and the fuel bottle go into side pockets, as does a water bottle and the water filter. The bottom compartment holds personal gear (I do take a book and a notebook), a small first aid kit put together after reading Dr. Bill Forgey's very comprehensive *Wilderness Medicine,* an extra match safe, a flashlight, a stubby candle in a tin, and some stuff that comes under the heading of *"health and beauty aids"* like toothbrush, toothpaste, bug dope, sunscreen, reading glasses, lip salve, needle and thread, another match safe, and toilet paper, all in a small stuff bag. A length of neatly reefed chute cord goes in here, too, for hanging up the food bag out of reach of critters.

I tend to be a *"compartment freak."* I like pockets in my packs (all but my canoe packs), and I like to keep things in stuff bags or heavy duty ziplocs inside the pack. It keeps me from losing things. It also lets me find things in a hurry, even in the dark. Why should I need to find things in the dark? Because I frequently walk in the dark, just as I frequently paddle in the dark. If you're going somewhere for a weekend, you can extend the useful time — time spent in the outback — by taking the first steps or strokes Friday night. And it raises an ordinary outing into the level of adventure as well. Things *do* go bump in the night out there! Person who says that the woods are quiet and peaceful ain't never been there, for certain sure!

Raingear stays under the pack flap, so it's easily accessible. Maps go into the header pocket on the pack flap. My compass goes into my shirt pocket, and my knife goes into my pants pocket and is secured by a lanyard. If I take a camera, I'll tether it to the packframe, where it's reasonably accessible. I don't usually take a camera except for *"record shots,"* because I've never been able to shoot seriously on a pleasure trip. If I seek photographs, I go out just for photographs. When I lived in New York State, I wouldn't have considered taking binoculars. Here in Michigan, the jackpine and cutover terrain is swarming with birds. Alas, my binoculars are both bulky and heavy, so I'm saving the bucks I used to spend buying tobacco and put them into a vest pocket pair of binocs that will truly live in a pocket and be *there* when I want them. Hey — you don't get many chances in this life to see a Kirtland's Warbler!

Some of this gear gets split up if Molly and I walk together. I'll slough off the tent poles on her, and perhaps the cookpots, but I'll take all the food. The idea is that no member of the party should be overburdened. I will NOT carry Molly's little square foam pillow, although I'll gladly boost it in the wee small hours. I use my lightweight pile jacket in the sleeping bag stuff sack as a pillow.

How much should all of this weigh? I'd like to keep the weight at or under 20% of my body weight, which is about 165 pounds. (Don't let anybody tell you that the weight you put once you pass 50 is muscle. I'm ten pounds above my best canoe racing weight, and it's all right there in front, looking at me.) This results in a pack of under 35 pounds, which is more than liveable. If your pack fits, and you need to do it in an emergency, you can carry half your body weight with no problem, but with no fun either. The key to that kind of packing — and the key to lightweight packing as well — is how you get the pack on and off your back.

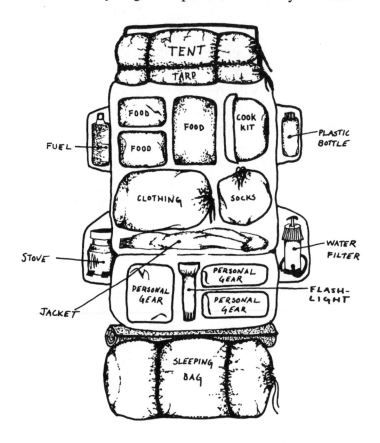

Figure 19   An example of a well organized pack. Clothing should include: extra socks, Polypro T-shirts, and pants. Personal gear should include a book, medical kit, writing pad, matches (waterproofed), flashlight, emergency candles, and hygienic items.

Load 'Em Up And Move 'Em Out. It's amazing what get perpetrated on the unsuspecting pilgrim with a backpack. For example, the backpacking public has been solemnly told that the easiest way to *"shoulder"* your burden (you really *"hip"* your burden, of course) is to sit down, kind of wiggle into the packstraps, and then just roll forward and stand up. What a wonderful way to do in your back and get a hernia at the same time!

Here's how to get into harness with a loaded pack.

I'm right-handed. If you're a lefty, you may want to switch sides, but I'm not sure it really matters. Unlatch the hipbelt. Loosen both shoulder straps. Pick the pack up with your right hand on the crossbar from which the shoulder straps are suspended and your left hand on the right-hand strap (*"right"* as it would be as you are wearing it.) Get the pack up high enough so you can support its weight mostly on your right knee. Now, slide your right arm and shoulder under the right hand shoulder strap, using your knee to boost the weight up. Grab the shoulder strap with your right hand somewhere around where the padded area meets the nylon webbing, and keep the pack from pivoting with your elbow. (It's easier than it sounds). Now, slip your left arm under the left-hand shoulder strap, roll your shoulders forward, and fasten the hip belt. Now tighten the shoulder straps and begin the ritual dance of loosening and tightening, wriggling and jiggling, to get everything settled in. Easy! Your leg does the heavy work; your arms position things more than lift things.

To get out of the pack, loosen the left shoulder strap, slide out of it, and then release the hipbelt. The pack will still be pretty solidly positioned on your right shoulder. Reach across your body with your left hand, grab the right shoulder strap, and simply turn out from under the pack, which will slide down onto your knee, from whence it can be slid down to the ground. It works. Try it a few times in the living room until it becomes second nature. The time to learn it is not when you're tired!

7. WOODSPERSONSHIP

There are always items that don't fit comfortably into neat categories. They're ways of seeing and ways of thinking rather than ways of doing, and sometimes they get lost or overlooked in the vast mass of *"how-to."* Let's chat about some of these things.

Basic Routefinding. This isn't a small textbook on map and compass work. For that, I cheerfully refer you to Cliff Jacobson's new book, *The Basic Essentials of Map & Compass,* another publication of ICS Books. Like all of Cliff's work, it's a model of clarity.

What I want to talk about with you is the simplest of all compass skills, and one you'll use almost exclusively when you take a random scoot in the woods. It's called *"walking a field bearing."* You don't need a map for it, but you obviously need a compass. The best kind is that style which is mounted on a plate. It's sometimes called an orienteering compass, although an orienteering compass is a specialized version of the base-plate unit.

Here's the situation. You're out in the hilly country that starts about twelve miles inland from Lake Huron in the northern part of Michigan's lower peninsula. You recognize the terrain for what it is — big sand dunes that formed along the shores of a much older Lake Huron. The land's been burned over frequently, and while it's easy walking, the scrub oak and jackpine are pretty thick. And most jackpines look alike. You've left your car along the road, and you want to roam a little. Great! When faced with that kind of impulse, yield to it. Your life will be richer for it.

So, you start, with your daypack and your compass. Before you go anywhere, point the direction of travel arrow at some prominent object in the direction toward which you're heading. It could be a distinctive tree, or maybe just what seems to be a cleared area in a hundred yards or so. Now, turn the dial of the compass — called a bezel in formal parlance, should you ever have to speak to a compass —until the red end of the magnetic needle points towards zero degrees. Now read your field bearing at the index on the dial. Keep the magnetic needle framed inside the orienting arrow on the bottom of the rotating bezel as a quick check on your bearing.

Now, start walking toward that first objective you sighted. When you get there, take another sighting along the bearing you've been walking, and walk to it. Simple, yes?

Well, it's simple until you drop down off one hillock and stare at a neat little bog that you'd rather not cross because you might sink out of sight. Stop and look. Most little bogs are not punchbowls of stagnant water; they're small, dying lakes. The term is eutrophic lake or bog, in case you're curious. There's an inlet and an outlet to this bog, and it should be no mystery to you that the inlet is on the *"high"* side of the bog. You're walking a bearing of 75 degrees already. Sight against some landmark and start walking. Take a moment to look back over your shoulder, though, to see where you were. This time, though, count every double step you take, just like the Roman legionnaires did. In other words, every time your left foot strikes the ground, you count. Record the number of paces (remember your Latin? Multi millia passuum?) in your little pocket notebook that always goes with you. When you arrive at the high side of the bog, turn left 90 degrees, and, lo and behold, you're back at your familiar 65 degree field bearing. Walk this bearing for long enough to clear the far side of the bog (counting your paces, of course), and turn left again. Now, you'll be walking a bearing of 65 degrees *minus* 90 degrees, or 345 degrees. (There are 360 degrees in a circle). Sight your objective, and follow this bearing for the same number of paces you took back when you turned right to avoid the bog. After you've done that, you should be directly opposite where you started from when your detour began. Turn right, back to your 65 degree bearing, sight against another landmark and start in walking again.

You may have to detour around several things, even on a very casual ramble, but if you make your turns 90 degrees, and keep track of your paces, you should be able to go into the bush for quite a while without a map and come back out again. You'll do this more easily if you take the time, at each turning and even when you're just walking that same old familiar bearing, to look around and familiarize yourself with the terrain. Don't look on this as a *"survival skill"* or any other sort of precious nonsense. You're out there to look around in the first place! Take the time to look, to see, in an unhurried fashion, and when you come back, the terrain will be familiar and friendly rather than foreboding and formidable.

Getting back is like getting out, but backwards. If we walked out at a field bearing of 65 degrees, we walk back at 65 plus 180, or 225 degrees. This is called a *back bearing,* and there's nothing at all mysterious about it.

However, you probably won't come out at exactly the same place on the road unless you've observed very carefully on the way in. You'll be close. In fact, you'll probably be right on the money when you leave the first bog you encountered. But, unless the road along which you left your car is pretty straight, chances are good that your car won't be in sight when you get out. This is no problem; it probably won't be over a quarter-mile off — *but in what direction?* Of course, at this point, it's always raining.

Here's what you do. When you arrive at that last known point, which in this case is the bog, cheat a little if you can't visualize the terrain exactly. Instead of walking out at 225 degrees, walk out at 230 degrees. You know that you won't wind up at your car, but you're sure to wind up a bit west of the car. Turn left, and your car will be there, just around the bend.

Simple, yes? Yes! And a simpler still if you take the time to look around — which is why you're out there in the first place!

Knives. Carry a pocket knife or a small sheath knife. You don't need a *"survival knife"* or any such stuff, because except for making a fuzz stick to start a fire on a wet day, the most dangerous thing you'll be stabbing is commercial peanut butter made with *hydrolized vegetable oil* and sugar. It goes without saying that a knife must be SHARP. I carry a small diamond whetstone in my *"health and beauty aids"* bag, and I view maintaining a good edge on the knife as a game to play while the water heats up.

Staying Found. Staying found is an attitude as well as a skill, and more people get lost on a casual walk than do on long trips. Why? The long trips are generally well planned. You're going with maps, and you're paying attention to them. Your map and compass skills are well-honed, and because this is a Big Trip, you're paying attention to your surroundings. That's the key. Take the time to turn around and see where you've been. Take the time to notice where the sun is as you walk. Be aware of your surroundings. You might not know exactly where you are — but you know where you came from. And that's all you need to know.

Sanitation. In simple terms, do not eliminate, wash, throw fish guts, or toss dishwater or uneaten food into any watercourse. Period. Go far away from camp for such functions, and leave whatever you leave behind in a shallow (2-3 inches deep at most) cathole, where all sorts of bacteria will dispose of it. Needless to add — but I'll add it anyway — everything else comes back out with you, and that includes junk some slobs have left. Carry a small plastic trash bag with you for this unpleasant but necessary function.

Leadership. Most backpackers rarely find themselves in a position where they're on a trip that requires formal leadership, so we won't talk about that. But any trip of any length with one other person is a leadership situation, or at least a situation in which decisions have to be made.

Nowhere is it written that the decision-maker must be the male in a party made up of one man and one woman. It may well be that the male has had more experience in the outback, but I remind you that a poor wine corked badly and aged for ten years is called vinegar. Guard against certain things, please. Do not EVER press people beyond their capacity in a recreational situation. That's not *"getting tough;"* that's getting clinically sadistic. Do not let recreational walks turn into situations that require a life or death effort by sheer carelessness or lack of observation. If you're soaked to the skin and shivering, don't press on. Make camp there, eat, get warm before you settle into hypothermia. And if one person shows signs of fatigue, hypothermia or heat stroke, don't insist on toughing it out. Make camp, or, if on a day hike, take care of the problem NOW before you have a full-blown emergency on your hands. In brief, don't play the boy/girl game; play the adult/adult game.

Walking With Kids and the Elderly. This is a leadership function that isn't nearly as heroic as you might envision in your fantasies, but which is probably the most important leadership function you'll every exercise.

Okay. I was a kid once. And I'm past 50, which, while it does not make me feeble, does give me a different agenda on a walk. In a very real sense, it's a kid's agenda. Kids and Gray Panthers are interested in the here and now, and singularly uninterested in goals. I wanted to soak it all up when I was a kid, and I want now to soak it all up because I might not travel this way again. When I was a younger man, though, the challenge was getting there — usually in a heck of a hurry. Hey — I had all of my life to putter around and smell the flowers!

So ... if you walk with children or the elderly, you will walk to the beat of a different drummer. You can relax and remember how it was when you were a kid. You can unwind and listen while Dad or Grandpa points out the difference between *Pinus banksiana* and *Pinus resinosa* to you for the twentieth time. But this time, maybe, it'll stick, and you can tell your kids.

A walk in the woods with the old and the young is a walk with no objective beyond the pleasure of the moment. There is no challenge to overcome, because a fringed gentian only offers beauty. And there is nothing at all to conquer except your own addiction to conquering.

Bring something special for lunch. Bring the bird book. Bring the wildflower book. Bring the binoculars. And bring an easy mind, secure and happy in the knowledge that this is not YOUR trip. Somebody else for whom you care very much. And if you don't get to that neat pond three ridges over, you'll probably get to somewhere you never knew existed until you saw it through wiser eyes than yours.

Enjoy.

Final Chortle. Smell the roses. Enjoy the view. Be kind to your companions and to the world you walk through. And if you see me in the woods or on a river, wave.

Annotated Equipment List
For A Walk In The Woods

1. Small pack. I prefer a compartmentalized teardrop for convenience.
2. Comfortable shoes or boots. Size them to fit a pair of heavy wool socks and lightweight liner socks.
3. Lightweight rain jacket with hood. The waterproof/breathable fabrics work well in this application; so does a simple coated nylon shell. Of late, I've been wearing a shell made of very light waxed cotton. It's British-made, quite expensive, drably functional, and very nearly perfect for the damp, windy Great Lakes coast.
4. Water bottle. Take a liter. Yes, it's heavy. You'll never notice the weight. Wrap it up in the rainshell to keep it cool.
5. Munchies. A hard roll, some cheese, and a few peanuts are well nigh perfect for me. It may not be for you. For a few hours in the woods, food is more of a consolation than a necessity. A pocket knife is part of the food pack.
6. Map and compass. Even if you don't need it, view it as a data bank and as a creator of enthusiasm for future walks. Also — the time to learn map and compass work is when you don't need to know it.
7. First aid kit. I honor this more in the abeyance, but a small kit and an ankle wrap is the way to fly. Keep both in your pack all the time, and you'll never leave them at home. Iodine tabs go in the kit. The same goes for:
8. Insect repellent and sunscreen. Keep them in your pack.
9. Field guides, notebook and pen. Your choice. We always have a bird guide, a wildflower guide, and a pair of binoculars with us, and frequently a tree guide as well, if we're out of familiar territory.
10. Toilet paper.

This is a very basic list. I have no doubt that most authorities would say that my safety equipment is very sparse, and no doubt it is. This is for a short jaunt in easy country. If you're walking in more rugged terrain, or in a trackless area, or in marginal weather, you might well augment this list with a lightweight pile jacket or polypro sweater, matches in a waterproof container, a Space blanket, and lightweight rain pants or rain chaps.

By now, you've outgrown your small pack, so take the rucksack off the wall (it has its own first aid kit, remember?) and be comfortable. If there's snow on the ground, beef up your footgear, take an extra pair of socks with you, staple your sunglasses to your ears, grab your shell mittens with wool mitten liners, and enjoy, enjoy, enjoy. You might even take a seed and suet cake with you for the chickadees and nuthatches.

An Annotated Equipment List for Overnighting

1. Frame pack and bag. Check all attachment points; rub the zippers with a candle, shake out the mice.
2. Tent. When was the last time the seams were sealed? Best do it now, because you can't do it at two in the morning when the wind is wailing and the rain is falling so hard it smokes. And you will check the poles and tent skewers, of course. Good!
3. Sleeping system. Sleeping bag, pillow if you need one, and a sleeping pad. I don't go out there to rough it; I carry a Therma-Rest, and laugh at the small extra weight.
4. Boots. If you're carrying your house on your back, you'll need something sturdier on your feet than tennies or running shoes. The rule's the same: heavy socks and liner socks.
5. Cooking gear. A small stove, a couple of pots, a pot lifter, a scrub pad and biodegradable soap, a tablespoon (all-purpose, for eating and mixing), and a cup. All the cookgear is clean, of course, and in its own stuff sack. And the stove has been checked over, and you packed the fuel in its own pack pocket? Of course! And you did throw in the little plastic bag of absolutely necessary stove parts?

6. Food. Your choice. I keep it simple, preferring to eat to live rather than live to eat, but I always take along something sinfully self-indulgent. Take enough for an extra day — and never assume you'll catch fish!

7. Water filter. First Need or Katadyn. The alternative has most unpleasant names: turistas, Montezuma's Revenge, the trots

8. Other stuff You'd Take On a Day Trip. Of course, you'll take the usual like the first aid kit, the ankle wrap, the pocket knife, the map, the compass, clothing to suit the weather, personal medication and such. I know that. What you need to think about is how much other stuff to take. You may want to trade the field guides for a small camera, or you may prefer to take all of them. You'll certainly take your 1-liter water bottle — and you may want another one for convenience in cooking. I do. Sometimes, I fill both and tote them along if I'm in "new" country, because I don't know where the water supplies are. And I won't overburden myself with a lot of extra clothes. Pounds for warmth and dryness; not one ounce for vanity. You can survive without a change of clothes for a weekend.

9. Flashlight. Candle lanterns are neat toys, and I usually take one, but a small flashlight (spare bulb inside) is the preferred working tool. The batteries are fresh, of course.

10. A relaxed mind. Roll with the punches, enjoy the rain.

APPENDIX 2

The Outdoor First Aid Kit

State-of-the-art dressings, wound closure tapes, and non-prescription medications allow the construction of a very useful first aid kit for general outdoor use.

This book has described various first aid procedures that frequently use the items listed in the following kit. Very often treatments can be improvised with other items on hand, but prior planning and the inclusion of these items in your kit will provide you with the best that modern medical science can offer.

This kit, and all of the individual components, are available from Indiana Camp Supply, as indicated below.

Quantity	Item
2 pkgs	Coverstrip Closures ¼" x 3" 3/pkg
1	Spenco 2nd Skin Dressing Kit
1	Bulb irrigating syringe
5 pkg	Nu-Gauze, high absorbent, sterile, 2 ply, 3" x 3" pkg/2

1	Surgipad, Sterile, 8" x 10"
2	Elastomull, Sterile Roller Gauze, 4" x 162"
2	Elastomull, Sterile Roller Gauze, 2½" x 162"
10	Coverlet Bandage Strips 1" x 3"
1	Tape, Hypoallergenic ½" x 10 YD
1	Hydrocortisone Cream .5%, 1 oz tube (allergic skin)
1	Triple Antibiotic Ointment, 1 oz tube (prevents infection)
1	Hibiclens Surgical Scrub, 4 oz (prevents infection)
1	Dibucaine Ointment 1%, 1 oz tube (local pain relief)
1	Tetrahydrozoline Ophthalmic Drops, (eye irritation)
1	Starr Otic Drops, ½ oz bottle (ear pain, wax)
1	Micronazole Cream, 2%, ½ oz tube (fungal infection)
24	Actifed Tablets (decongestant)
24	Mobigesic Tablets (pain, fever, inflammation)
24	Meclizine 25 mg tab (nausea, motion sickness prevention)
2	Ammonia Inhalants (stimulant)
24	Benadryl 25 mg cap (antihistamine)
10	Bisacodyl 5 mg (constipation)
25	Diasorb (diarrhea)
25	Dimacid (antacid)
2 pkg	Q-tips, sterile, 2 per package
1	Extractor Kit (snake bite, sting, wound care)
6	1 oz Vials for repackaging the above
1	Over-pak Container for above

Consideration should be given to a dental kit. Several are commercially available through backpacking and outdoor outfitters. As a minimum, a small bottle of oil of cloves can serve as a topical toothache treatment or a tube of toothache gel can be obtained. A fever thermometer should be included on trips. People wearing contact lenses should carry suction cup or rubber pincher device to aid in their removal. An adequate means of water purification must also be arranged.

Additional modules to this kit are described in detail in *Wilderness Medicine*, reference 5, some of which include prescription level medications. The above kit, and the advanced treatment modules, can be purchased pre-packed, and /or the individual items may be purchased separately from Indiana Camp Supply, Inc., PO Box 211, Hobart, Indiana 46342 — telephone (219) 947-2525.

APPENDIX 3

AHS CLUB AFFILIATES

The Adirondack Mountain Club
174 Glen Street
Glens Falls, NY 12801

The Adirondack 46'ers
RFD 1, Box 390
Morrisonville, NY 12962

Adventures for Women, Inc.
P.O. Box 515
Montvale, NJ 07645

Appalachian Long Distance
  Hikers Assoc.
RD 2, Box 194
Kempton, PA 19529

Appalachian Mountain Club
5 Joy Street
Boston, MA 02108

Appalachian Trail Conference
P.O. Box 807
Harpers Ferry, WV 25425

Berkeley Hiking Club
Box 147
Berkeley, CA 94701

Blue Mountain Eagle
  Climbing Club
P.O. Box 3523
Reading, PA 19605

Buckeye Trail Association
P.O. Box 254
Worthington, OH 43085

C & O Canal Association
P.O. Box 166
Glen Echo, MD 20812

Cascadians
P.O. Box 2201
Yakima, WA 98097

Center Hiking Club
4608 Coachway Drive
Rockville, MD 20852

Central Arizona Backpackers
5 S. Pleblo St.
Gilbert, AZ 85234

Central Ohio Hiking Club
% YMCA / 40 W. Long St.
Columbus, OH 42215

Genesee Valley Hiking Club
94 Sunset Trail W
Fairport, NY 14450

Greenville Hiking Club
Rt. 3, Box 274
Chuckey, TN 37641

Huachuca Hiking Club
3705 Shawnee Drive
Sierra Vista, AZ 85635

Iowa Trails Council
1201 Central
Center Point, IA 52213

La Canada Flintridge
  Trails Council
P.O. Box 852
La Canada Flintridge, CA 91011

Loxahatchee Chapter FTA
P.O. Box 19393
W. Palm Beach, FL 33406-9393

Mason Dixon Trail System
P.O. Box 116
Kennett Square, PA 19348

Michigan Trailfinders Club
2680 Rockhill NE
Grand Rapids, MI 49505

Minnesota Rovers Outing Club
P.O. Box 14133
Minneapolis, MN 55414

The Mountaineers
300 Third Ave. West
Seattle, WA 98119

Natural Bridge ATC
P.O. Box 3012
Lynchburg, VA 24503

New York Section/Green
  Mountain Club
250 DeGraw Avenue
Teaneck, NJ 07666

NY/NJ Trail Conference
232 Madison Ave.
New York, NY 10016

North Country Trail Association
P.O. Box 311
White Cloud, MI 49349

Chatham Trails Association
37 Clinton Street
Concord, NH 03301

Cleveland Hiking Club
2508 Portman Ave.
Cleveland, OH 44109

Colorado Mountain Club
2530 W. Alameda Ave.
Denver, CO 80210

Continental Divide Trail Soc.
P.O. Box 30002
Bethesda, MD 20814

Contra Costa Hills Club
125 - 12th St. #104
Oakland, CA 94607

Desert Trail Association
P.O. Box 589
Burns, OR 97720

Diablo Hiking Club
1580 Lexington Road
Concord, CA 94520

Finger Lake Trail Conference
P.O. Box 18048
Rochester, NY 14618

Florida Trail Association
P.O. Box 13708
Gainesville, FL 32604

Foothills Trail Club
13781 Fish Hill Rd.
South Wales, NY 14129

Tidewater Appalachian
  Trail Club
P.O. Box 8246
Norfolk, VA 23503

Triple Cities Hiking Club
P.O. Box 22
Johnson City, NY 13790

Trails Club of Rossmoor
2665 Pine Knoll Dr.
Walnut Creek, CA 94595

Virginia Tech Outing Club
Virginia Poly Tech Institute
Blacksburg, VA 24061

Virginia Trails Association
13 West Maple Street
Alexandria, VA 22301

North Star High Adventure Team
3179 Napa Drive
San Jose, CA 95148

Old Dominion ATC
P.O. Box 25283
Richmond, VA 23260-5283

Ozark Highlands Trail Association
P.O. Box 1074
Fayetteville, AR 72703

Pacific Northwest Trail Association
P.O. Box 1048
Seattle, WA 98111

Penn State Outing Club/Hiking Div.
Rm, 4 Intramural Bldg.
University Park, PA 16802

Potomac Appalachian Trail Club
1718 N Street NW
Washington DC 20036

Rails-To-Trails Conservancy
1400 - 16th St. N.W.
Washington DC 20036

Roanoke ATC
6913 Bradshaw Ave.
Salem, VA 24153

Superior Hiking Trails Association
Box 2157
Tofte, MN 55615

Susquehanna ATC
P.O. Box 215
Harrisburg, PA 17108-0215

The Vulcan Trail Association Inc.
P.O. Box 31104
Birmingham, AL 35222

Washington Trails Association
1305 Fourth Ave. #518
Seattle, WA 98101

Wilmington Trail Club
P.O. Box 1184
Wilmington, DE 19899

Wisconsin Go-Hiking Club
5556 N. 103 St.
Milwaukee, WI 53225

Index